Irving Berlin's GOLDEN YEARS

Volume 2

D0896214

First Published 1983
© International Music Publications

Exclusive Distributors
International Music Publications
60/70 Roden Street, Ilford, England

215-2-125

ALEXANDER'S RAGTIME BAND

Words and Music by IRVING BERLIN

land,............ They can play a bu‑gle call like you nev‑er heard be‑fore,

So nat‑ur‑al that you want to go to war; That's just the

best‑est band what am, hon‑ey lamb, Come on a‑

long,................ Come on a‑long,................ Let me take you by the

BACK TO BACK

Words and Music by IRVING BERLIN

THE BEST THINGS HAPPEN WHILE YOU'RE DANCING

Words and Music by IRVING BERLIN

CHOREOGRAPHY

Words and Music by IRVING BERLIN

EVERYBODY'S DOING IT NOW!

Words and Music by IRVING BERLIN

13

GET THEE BEHIND ME SATAN

Slowly, but Rhythmic

Words and Music by IRVING BERLIN

HE AIN'T GOT RHYTHM

Words and Music by IRVING BERLIN

I THREW A KISS IN THE OCEAN

Words and Music by IRVING BERLIN

Lyrics:
You'll say it's a dream, a love-ly dream___
I say it hap-pened, strange as it may seem.

CHORUS

I spoke last night to the o-cean _____ I spoke last night to the sea. _____ And from the o-cean a voice came back 'Twas my Blue Jack-et an-swer-ing me. _____ Ship a-

I WANT TO BE IN DIXIE

Words and Music by IRVING BERLIN

or for - sak - en Sun-ny land of cot - ton down to the town I was
train is near - in' Dear old Dix - ie, bet - ter shout, hol - ler out, good and
F7 F11 F+ B♭
born, Im glad I had Im glad I had E-nough to
loud. Con-duc-tor man Con-duc-tor man I'm goin' to
F9 B♭ F7 B♭ F7
buy a tick - et Now I hope that there will be no pause
fall a - sleep now, Tell the mo - tor man to start the train
B♭ B♭m F F♯0
Let me tell...... you the rea - son is be - cause:
Let me tell...... you when I wake up a - gain:
Gm C7 F7 E♭(F) A♭m6 F7

I'LL SEE YOU IN C-U-B-A

Words and Music by IRVING BERLIN

Moderato con moto

Not so far from here, There's a ve-ry
Take a friend's ad-vice, Drink-ing in a

live-ly at-mos-phere, Ev'-ry-bo-dy's go-ing there this
cel-lar is-n't nice, An-y-bo-dy who has got the

IT ONLY HAPPENS WHEN I DANCE WITH YOU

Words and Music by IRVING BERLIN

OH! HOW IT HATE TO GET UP IN THE MORNING

Words and Music by IRVING BERLIN

The oth - er day I chanced to meet a

A bu - gler in the ar - my is the

CHORUS

THE PICCOLINO

Words and Music by IRVING BERLIN

42

(DANCE TO THE MUSIC OF)
THE OCARINA

Words and Music by IRVING BERLIN

Medium Polka Tempo

Verse

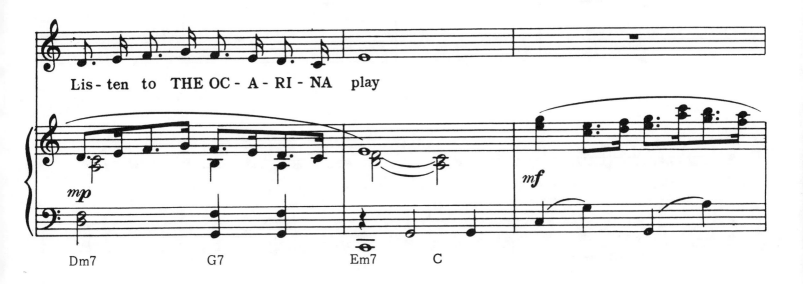

Lis - ten to THE OC - A - RI - NA play

Lis - ten, don't you seem to hear it say;

THE SONG OF THE METRONOME

Words and Music by IRVING BERLIN

but you will last ___ Bet-ter to be late than to not ar-rive *Tick - tock*

Tick - tock Four o'-clock has gone but you still have five *Tick - tock* *Tick - tock*

When your day is ov-er you'll be up-on the shelf, So broth-er, dont run a - way with yourself, Don't run a-way from THE

SONG OF THE MET - RO - NOME ___ -NOME ___

A SAILOR'S NOT A SAILOR
('Til A Sailor's Been Tattooed)

Words and Music by IRVING BERLIN

WHEN I LEAVE THE WORLD BEHIND

Words and Music by IRVING BERLIN

WHEN I LOST YOU

Words and Music by IRVING BERLIN

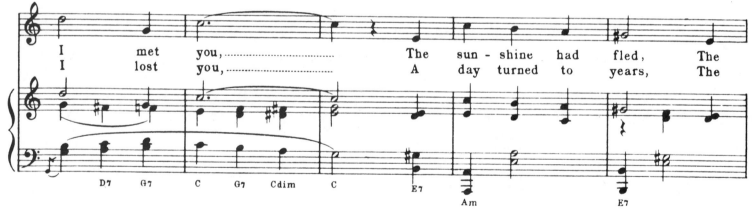

CHORUS

WHEN THE MIDNIGHT CHOO-CHOO LEAVES FOR ALABAM'

Words and Music by IRVING BERLIN

up my drea-ry flat,........... Where many wea-ry nights I sat, Think - ing
kiss my Pa and Ma .... A doz-en times for ev'-ry star, Shin - ing

Eb   Bb+   Eb   Bb+   Eb Eb6 Gb7

of the folks down home who think of   me:... You can
o - ver Al - a - ba-ma's new mown hay;... I'll be

Bb E⁰ F7 Bb Cm Ab F6 F7 Bb Ebm Bb Ebm Bb   Bb7

bet you'll find me sing - ing hap-pi - ly...........................
glad e - nough to throw my - self a - way...........................

Ab/Bb Bb7   Ab/Bb Bb7

CHORUS

When the mid - night choo - choo leaves for Al - a - bam',...........................

p-f

Eb   Eb   C Fm Bb7   Eb

YOU CAN HAVE HIM

Words and Music by IRVING BERLIN

YOU KEEP COMING BACK LIKE A SONG

Words and Music by IRVING BERLIN

YOU'D BE SURPRISED

Words and Music by IRVING BERLIN

CHORUS *2nd time f*

Tacet
G
D9
D13

- prised ____ He is-n't much at a dance but then when he takes you home,
- prised ____ He is-n't much in the light but when he gets in the dark,

You'd be sur-
You'd be sur-

D7   D9   D7   D9   D7   G

- prised ___ He does-n't look like much of a lov - er, but don't judge a book by its cov - er;
- prised ___ I know he looks so slow and so wea - ry, but you don't know the half of it, dear - ie;

D7 G7 C   Em7 Cm6   G   E7+ E7

He's got the face of an an - gel, but
He looks as cold as an Es - ki - mo,

There's a dev - il in his eyes ____ He's such a
But there's fire in his eyes ____ He does-n't

A7   A9 A7   D9   G D7 Am7 D7 Tacet

I LEFT MY HEART AT
THE STAGE DOOR CANTEEN

Words and Music by IRVING BERLIN

See page 74 for Introduction and Verse

REFRAIN Slowly with expression

I left my heart at the Stage Door Can - teen ___ I left it

there with a girl named Eil - een. ___ I kept her serv-ing

doughnuts 'til all she had were gone, I sat there dunking doughnuts 'til she caught

Slowly with expression

Old Mis-ter Ab-sent-mind-ed that's me _____ Just as for-

F   Fdim   Gm   F

-get-ful as I can be. _____ I've got the strangest sort of a

Dm   Gm   C7   F   Bb   A7

Back to Refrain

mind, _____ I'm al-ways leav-ing something be - hind. _____

Dm   G9   C7 Cdim C7

WHO DO YOU LOVE I HOPE

Words and Music by IRVING BERLIN

REFRAIN *with a lift*

Who do you love_ I hope? Who would you kiss I hope?

Who is it go-ing to be_____ I hope, I hope, I hope it's me._

Who do you want I hope? Who do you need I hope?

Who is it go-ing to be?_____ I hope, I hope, I hope it's me._

I'M AN INDIAN TOO

See page 80 for Introduction and Verse

Words and Music by IRVING BERLIN

INTRODUCTION and VERSE

Moderately bright

Since I was a child of three, they've had the In-di-an sign on me, they'd sit and watch me as I grew_____ I would dream how nice 'twould be to have an In-di-an fam-i-ly and now my dreams have all come true._____

Back to Refrain